Circuitry

Patrick Mackay

JAKE BOOKS 2012

Circuitry, copyright © 2012, **Jake Books**

CATALOG

Your Majesties
The Crystal Set
Perfect Entropy
Deadpan
Experimental Music
The Book of Jake
The No Theater
Circuitry

ISBN 0-9678151-9-3

Contents

Your Majesties

Relinquishment   6
Laying Stone   7
The War on TV   9
Good Night Moon   10

The Crystal Set

Preface   12
Marble Day   16
To Hear Other Worlds   18
Paper Airplanes   19
Below the Frequency of Light   21
The Letter   24
The Resilience of Grass   25

Perfect Entropy

Last Things Said   28
Caroline's Grave   30
Sketches of Pelicans   32
Circuitry   34
Anti Psychotics   36
Evolution of a Fine Artist   38
Perfect Entropy   40
Gambling   42
The Chain Gang   45
Upon the Tracks   46
New Years Eve 2001/2   49
Changlings   52

Deadpan

Nouning Around   56
Eleven Different Ways to Understand Patience   57
Wasting Time in a Poem   59
Like You Know   61
Cell Phone   65
A Woman's Room   67
Kneading a Loaf of Bread   69

Experimental Music

Foreword   72
Anger   74
Fear   76
Desire   78
Panic   80
Greed   82
Depression   84
Anxiety   86
The Vocabulary of Dopamine   88
1   90
A Minute of Your time   92
5:23pm   93

The No Theater

Leftovers   96
Lake Missing   98
Deep   99
When Nothing's There   101

Your Majesties

Relinquishment

My love is great
I cannot see
Her voice relinquishes
Me in me.

Naked truth
Takes its time
To trust
Where it opens from.

Ache within
I will hold
Make love's weight
Into gold.

Laying Stone

The ground under the pepper tree was mottled:
seeds, weeds, leaves, adventitious roots bulged up
showing me slow toil, the curled brown knuckles
of an ancient thing upon which I would work.

I lay into it with the shovel, sweat
and blister salting my hands, digging so
that it would be level; each stroke deeply cut,
and when it cut, I opened too.

I spread the sand over like icing sweet
that smelled of the rawness of once rivers,
the mull of mountains, broken rocks down deep,
a library of sediment that I read
with rake and shovel; and each scrape it said,
"I have been here for years, more years then years".

The Arizona flagstone looked like sunset,
slabs of dappled orange, streams of yellow
and when I scored it with the hammer it
split chips over my face, upon my brow,
until it cracked in half down the middle
and I lugged it up (sunset and all).

But placement has always been a puzzle
when Nature is put in the hands of man.

So I let them place themselves, my muscle
straining under the weight of them;
and they made up their own mosaic
that seemed by each something unique.

After, I stepped back and surveyed our work,
somehow a patio had formed itself.
Was I the tool, conductor, or was it luck?
I looked upon them startling myself—
there they were, firm, aged, rock-sure, solid,
and when I stood on them I was sure I stood.

The War on TV

"The advent of the machine has destroyed the direct relation between a man's intention and his deed. If St. George meets the dragon face to face and plunges a spear into its heart, he may legitimately say "I slew the dragon," but if he drops a bomb on the dragon from an altitude of twenty thousand feet, though his intention—to slay it—is the same, his act consists in pressing a lever and it is the bomb, not St. George, that does the killing."

We blew the bridge. No, we blew the train
On the bridge and imagination
Blew us too far away from the death.
No, it blew itself up in after shots,
Pictures blown up on televisions. No,
It blew the charred bodies so black
We didn't notice. No, we noticed, but felt
Nothing. No, we cringed and dealt
Cards, not thinking of it. No, it wasn't us
Blown on the bridge trying to get out.
No, they didn't notice either before
It happened. It was a channel. It was
Program. It was a show. No, it was, it wasn't, was it…
It was.

Good Night Moon

Stand in the kitchen and drink a glass of water
With the lights off save for your moon.
Find the trickle brilliant the alter
From day to night, past your afternoon.

Think back to when you were a child,
The accent upon your diaphanous skin,
Where the slight trickle tilts undefiled;
A drop from your lip hangs from your chin.

And kiss once with an extended tongue,
Your place of history like no other place.
Such evening, the evening then, alights with song,
The dripping faucet leaks a star's light in space.

Here you are barren of all life's pursuits.
The kitchen quivers with the refrigerator
And your back tingles sending spinal roots
Up to night's gloss of moon to liberate or

Simply to be alone away from all moving things.
No one knows that you are here
Except midnight as she unfolds her wings
And you drink from the celestial sphere.

The Crystal Set

Introduction

This work has evolved from the 'outside' in part. It was the poet Jack Spicer who first introduced me to such phenomenon—the Crystal Set; through his Vancouver lectures given in 1965—a title that is too much to bear alone, as it needs the musical accompaniment of a ghost orchestra passing through our strange world to properly understand Logos and to interpret the beauty of a our cluttered attics of desire.

My first thought was that I would base the text upon a recipe of history dating to 1901, the date of the first transatlantic wireless transmission from Cornwall to Cape Cod. This is interesting because it proved that we can fly 'in-words' and that the machines that we manufacture may be tools that can take us into some graceful beyond; a home that depends on the vitality of awareness as we encounter difference. Yet, more simply, this is a rather formal book for children who want to remember that 'we are here' always for them and that they create for us our future as we drift into this rather hard life.

It is difficult to say how "the best words in the best order" find themselves. My experience is that sensibility in this respect is a matter of being engrossed enough in the process to let it take you over. (Friends do help a great deal). Some may think being taken over is absurd and, of course, it is, as we see so many hostile takeovers in our still imperialistic society. But we must find the appropriate metaphors to properly see around the many objects of the world. Simply, if we are to 'bear across the stream' of life well, we must be open enough to allow our histories the measures of dialectic that gives them their respect and the respect of others.

Since I believe that it is history that largely determines the future, it becomes imperative to remember your own, despite the many distractions fascinating us away from proper interpretation of life. Hence the many poems about childhood. Then, if you are lost you will find that this text is an adventure that allows growth of the spirit as you tumble through the woods in some pitch of night. Is it true that Pegasus will deviate from the track in such a way? I think so. Just trust the steed to fly you through the enchantments.

You will find within *The Crystal Set* a number of styles: Free verse, Sestina, Villanelle, Quatrain, Terza Rima, Couplets, and an odd mixing of Haiku within the stanzas of the last Lullaby. It was Judson Jerome who first turned me on to thinking that "the only good verse is metered verse." Some may be startled if they do not go directly to the dictionary and discover that meter is a vital root of: 'moral', 'medical', metrical. Originally the meter carried the oral traditions along the back roads of the world and informed the masses of the pleasures of remembering well, via song and story telling. This is not to say that new forms of language should go unrecognized. They will emerge, and if they embody some structural integrity then their life spans will be much longer. One hopes that this is so; that we encounter the new with the same respect with which we support the old.

When I first found the channel in 1989, I knew that I was feeling an important experience that would present many challenges. To say the least, it took many years of being 'sick with the written word' before I actually sprouted from the loam of poetic misinterpretation to a little view of understanding this genre of art. Even now, I am dwarfed in comparison to the many masterful writers in the world and, in a way, I always hope to be. I remember Marc Berger first telling me that there are two ways to go. "Baby, you can go the hard way or you can go the easy way. IF you go the easy way then you only know how to go the easy way. If you go the hard way, you not only know how to go the hard way, but you know how to go the easy way that much better."

Since life, for many, is often unbearable, and we only endure by some tenuous thread of belief, it must be one of poetry's tasks to 'lead forth'. Simply, this means that a bad poem may have great content, but a good one after enduring the hardship of becoming will be: didactic, inspiring, visionary, sound, and will have a measure of humor for the lay man and the professional. If it is true that humor is intelligence, we must allow the tragedies of life to—like oysters who suck up the dross of the sea—produce a pearl in the end for mental sustenance and our on going characters of learning.

It was Alexander Pope who said that the more we understand the more mountains there will be. It is hard to love this statement immediately. One may think of the arduous climb of Sisyphus up the hill only to have his boulder roll back down again. Or better, our many climbs up into the aether as we attempt the impossible. What one is left with is a vision of verdant hills, rolling green moors, fresh air, and the accompaniment of a flock of rag a tag sheep bleating to the trees. This, in my opinion, is all that one could ask for, unless they were complex as hell, which of course our life is at times.

To return to some form of original question will arise, I hope, via a thorough reading of *The Set*. Since there really is no knob to turn unless you know how to turn in verse, the station this will be playing on is a serious problem, one I hope that will be tender enough to the good reader to not completely blow their head off, as Emily Dickenson once said. One question that may arise is how does Nature (or birth) live after a body has read a book? Since this requires that we appreciate art and read it with the same passion with which the author wrote it,

14

the passage will nurture you if it is well wrought. And I do not mean to be so arrogant as to say that this is a well-wrought book, it really is not. It just occurred as naturally as a surprise pregnancy!

Suffice to say that it was great fun creating *The Crystal Set*, an enjoyment that would not have arisen if I had not suffered well earlier. Ultimately, I present to you a very simple treatment of my past and my interests currently as one discovers that even a leaf falling from a tree may guide them to some form of natural calendar. I now hear the waves crashing upon some distant shoreline on a planet far away that nobody has named yet to take it away.

PDM
June 15, 2001

Marble Day

We were released by spring, the weather lighting
Our footsteps in the playground yard,
And it was marble season, that exciting

Clicking sound as the cat's eye hit the cherry boulder
That we reveled in as we played the part
Of a professional marble holder.

Bird cages, peewees, solids, all
Were kept in tube socks, but pick one out
And make your thumb into a spring, then pull

It back and fillip the thing and it rolls
On the black tarmac to the gleeful shout
Of success. Some looked like burning coals

Inside, others were pitch dark like night,
And for all we knew we were in a dream
As we pinballed around the yard, our sight

Set on cleaning house, at least getting one,
The shot and sudden kissing sound deemed
A hit. Above, the grandest marble of all, the sun,

Shone down and glowed the yard like promise.
A slight wind librated the leaves around

As we all entered the game, marble bliss

Burning in our children's eyes. And when you hit
One there was the seriousness that made no sound,
But had us, like gamblers, focusing on it,

Making sure that we collected the right amount,
As cats eyes wizzed and knocked another
Between the legs that were scissored out.

Click, tip, clack, sit, wit, smack, get it, flip
These sounds were sounds of pure joy
A chorus be-mingled with children's lips

Blossoming into daytime laughter,
The yard of running feet, the small round toy,
Thumbnail sized that now mattered

More than anything to us. And to us
The world that day had disappeared,
Wiped out completely by the rush

We felt, the elation flowing neatly
In our veins, the marbles flowing even neater
As we thumbed them out, as we

Rolled them, clipped the still ones
Into heaven, dirty with the glory of the ground
Laughing, laughing, laughing, laughing.

To Hear Other Worlds

I put a stethoscope up to the flowers
And heard last year's bees landing.
The petal runways were a glory of colors,
The air of summer hot and branding,
Sun at noon blazing into the tender eyes;
Let me see everything here that nature tries.

In each bud a thimble sized well
Filled with nectar and nighttime dew
Every part working down to the cell,
The minutia shaping worlds we never view
But depend on the same as pollination;
Let this garden be the sovereign nation.

The white butterflies stutter above the blooms
Like fingerprints if they could fly through the air,
The delicate wings, miniature moons
That occasionally shake the buds aware,
Like punctuation shaping a sentence;
Let this be poetry that the garden invents.

I put a stethoscope up to the flowers
And heard last years bees landing.
The swarming hive of summer powers
A-buzz like sandpaper on wood sanding
Life down to its raw elements;
Let this day hold these small remnants.

Paper Airplanes

The palm fronds wag in the wind slow
Like seaweed moving to ocean swells,
Each finger casting a shadow below.
In the distance the chiming clock bells

Tinge the air with soft noise,
And there on the tower all the birds
Are shaken from their stock-still poise.

Suddenly a memory of paper planes
Folded diligently so every crease
Was hope and the folding paper games
We used to play caught the street

On fire with promise. You hold it
Between index and thumb, eyes landing
On some extant vision of possibility that beyond
Captures you as you hold in your hand the thing

That will fly the day past all the hours.
Your hand draws back and the wind comes
Then the unknowing release as all the powers
In the world converge upon

This instant of flying. You see the invisible
Keep her in the air for a length of dreams

That depend completely on the indivisible
Attentions of the sky. At least it seems

To be this way. She flies one hundred feet
Of exhilaration and then softly settles down
And you run to a heaven in the street
That is magical, intoxicatingly your own.

Below the Frequency of Light

Consider

The butterfly wing: the up-in-the-air
Flutter, the delicacy right
In the spread venation, membranous
With colored scales just like
Sunsets: satellite dish diaphanous,
The thin of a veiled fog bank, crystal
Wear in the sky. Consider this fragile

Articulation between the wings
And thorax, high teetering just
Above petals, touch down kissing
Stamens, draw of nectar from the thimble
Sized well, perch and shake of trust
Entranced by the sweet, lit up flower
Runways. You see her here innocent,
Stutter, "the meek shall inherit the earth," and still
Something else is happening.

Consider now below the frequency of light
The radio wave as it passes through her wing,
Shudders, spectrum bending the components
Of thought—our broadcasts, that vocal
Sustenance of relationships, reaching
And quivering on the median veins,

Slipping and vibrating on the coastal
Margin—our words oddly flung into this occupant
Of the earth. Consider these mediums.

Does the wing beat them through
Or do they beat through the wing?
Do they wage waves of dissonance
Or do they fulfill, massage as vibration
Of voice might massage a fetus in the womb? Then,

Does she feel it when that old Churchill's
"Blood, sweat and tears" pass through,
G. Marconi's trans-Atlantic 's',
Hitler's inflamed voice raging against
Humanity, broadcasts of dog-eared ships
Going down in other worlds of time?

Do the wings quiver as some thoroughfare
Of our dealings, of our wants, of our slip-
Freudian-carnivaled tongue and cheeking,
New Years and ticket-tape parades
And Babe Ruth smacking another home?
Does she feel that crack of the bat as it
Infects the announcer's voice with excitement?

The butterfly lands and memory's full of us
Like buds broadcast invisibly through air,
Like ghosts on the edge of becoming flesh again,
Shudders through her, a billion voices that once:
Told the world, informed, guided, arrested
Made, relinquished, transformed, tested,

Relieved, vanquished, decided, held, delivered,
Shaped, loved, felt, sparked, inflamed, severed,
Distorted, believed, granted, solicited,
Created, dismembered, dreamed, covered—
All of this passes through and the world

Holds us all like a precious message,
Our bodies shaking against the unknown cold.

The Letter

For Arthur Denton

The day didn't keep within his eyes.
Blindness had settled deep like coals,
Yet he wrote the letter by heart's light.

Age, how you've come and laid demise,
The struggling builds and un-builds souls.
The day didn't keep within his eyes

Nor sun even though in youth we size
Ourselves up like brilliant heroes.
Yet he wrote the letter by heart's light.

Light, perhaps, like Milton knew, was inside.
Those who see this kind are the noble,
But the day didn't keep within his eyes.

Some have walked a million miles
And others failed, sank in the darker swells,
But he wrote the letter by heart's light.

What holds is that hidden strength of those who try.
Done it! he said, victory and from there he grows.
Though the day didn't keep within his eyes
He wrote that letter by heart's light.

The Resilience of Grass

It is hard to imagine something as
Resilient as grass.

One hundred and eighty pounds of human
And it still bounces back.

Five hundred and thirty pounds of fat cows
It seems to hold the day.

Have a hundred people over for a party
And watch her hold the weight.

Roll bowling balls across the green,
Put cleats on and play the game.
Take the mower out and cut,
Yet she always grows again.

Spill alcohol upon her stems,
Lay reclining chairs and lie out.
Forget to water her, no rain,
And she always comes about.

And we have so many dreams that make up
Who we are,

Imagine what it would be like if they were grassier!

Hack and cut, chop and step, mow it to the ground,
Yet the grass simply lies there and always comes around.

Perfect Entropy

Last Things Said

For Arthur

He makes his tea with trembling fingers,
Dusk in his eyes where blindness lingers
So all the shapes round the room are shadows.

It used to be another way. He was the driver
Of a London bus, red double-decker, full no less.
And he drove holding the wheel like this.

It used to be that he did not have to
Navigate using a cane with you
Around the house.

He was the man who laid all his own piping,
Painted his home, put in the siding,
Electrical wires, knobs, hoses.

Now his heroism is in his letters, that is,
He writes even though his blindness
Prevents him, disposes.

I watch him and think over the years
Those things we did: Happy New Years!
Every day, every toast.

I watch him now and we pretend

That this time there is no end
To ourselves.

He was the man who took the mick
And knew every kind of verbal trick
To get you going.

He was the one who said bugger all
And attracted every robust call
Of the women.

But now we wander in old age,
Have been taken off the stage
And quit it then.

Dear Grandpa, you must know this,
That even though we are men I kiss
Your cheek.

And let the last things be said,
All your dreams now in your head,
Sleep well, sleep.

Caroline's Grave

Deep purple Magnolia flowers
Where my grandmother is buried
That you can see from the porch.

They bloom in winter's silent powers,
Having traveled from England, carried—
As death will us later—now a lighted torch.

The fertile ground where we are married
To afterlife presents itself here in the scorch
Of buds that remember for us how her

Lips spoke, how her hands gestured, or,
How we now live without her body
That once danced in the room as much

As the wind now dances with them. See,
We are, at death, the beautiful memories
Made of petals and tears and the touch

That has faded into the well and stamen for
Birds to drink from. She seems in these
Magnolias to hold out her hands, erupting

As plants erupt from their silent toil up,
Trying to fit the sky in the same as she

Once fit into our family her laughter

At the absurd, her wisdom in her stories,
Her crying at every airport, all of her
Now kept within a bloom that we may look

To and see and feel when we think she's
In the room still cooking at the stove, or
Still talking about times passed that

Have scored our eyes with its fingers,
Telling us that it is ok to die just as
It is ok to change living into a flower.

Then, on Spring days when we are closer
To forgetting than we should be,
My mother takes the trowel out

And goes down and digs in, talking,
Nurturing, exclaiming about how
Things are on this side, all the stuff

That she can only explain to flowers.
And if there be response it will be
Silently felt as the garden growing up,

And death will tell her we live but
Never die really, we just live differently
Than before, as if a world without hours.

Sketches of Pelicans

1

These pelicans look like musical notes upon a bar.
All in a line, some higher, some lower than
Others. The wind plays them this way far out
Enough to believe they'll make it wherever
They are going. A bar of music, say,
Played in Aves major: feather
Undaunted by the weather, long bills
Like shovels to dig the ether. My
Approach would be the same
If I could sing.

2

You would not notice a 'V'
In the sky unless you
Were a poet, the shape of
This group, and the perfect
Symmetry of their silence.

An 'L' sometimes if they
Get it right, or have settled
Into wavering.

And I say, 'O' let's see

You do that my bright birds.
And since nothing is in order, they,
Having ridden a wave, settle

On the shore in an 'E'
Type of way and I
Look at them and say, "my,
What LOVE."

Circuitry

For Jack

The world is a broken machine
And we live in the circuitry
Making love to lose ourselves.

On the hard drive of the heart
None can feel the electric pain.
We smile a facade of riddles:

Who are you, who are really?
Language is the child that dreams
That he could mend the world

Playing the game for him made by us.
He plays and forgets and plays
Like the surface of a pond

Reflecting the sky, while the rain
Distorts him into bliss.
The rings of his tears are circuitry.

We make a game up to destroy time,
As if it could save us from time,
But a loop always brings us back.

We download our desires into the wreck

And wait in lines for our freedom.
The child plays with who he thinks we are,

But we are not ourselves. The screen
Illuminates only parts of us, the face
Shows only a mirror and the pain

Is as deep as a canyon and echoes
Within our want the same
As fine font that makes us smile.

No one wants to know what is really
Happening. The world is a broken machine
And we live in the circuitry.

Anti Psychotics

The deep song-synthetic enters my brain
In the form of a pill to keep me sane,
    Keep me.
Dreams become glue-thick, stick to my day,
But sorrow is not washed completely away
    Neatly.

Pain reverts as memory is washed,
The limbs shiver, storm lashed
    To the mast.
Heaviness sets in, weighs on the eyes,
Like fallen angels you learn to despise
    To get past.

And to think they don't know the long term affects,
Have only tested this a few years at best
    Doubts you.
Puts you into a more nervous state,
Like when originally stricken so all the dates
    Cloud you.

And to understand truly what drugs mean,
The prescribed-for-obedience-normalcy,
    Destroys trust.
You sit in the back seat of your life,
While everyone else gets it right,
    Goes for bust.

So insane, so difficult to measure it out,
Life becomes a fading in and out
	Like a static channel.
The drugs may save, happiness be had,
But you lose your suffering that made the add,
	Angelic rambles.

Slip now into the wheel of the world,
Fit in the thought that what matters is gold,
	Get on the track.
You have been fixed and slotted, groomed again,
You can smile and save yourself from love's pure pain
	But not go back.

Evolution of a Fine Artist

For Brendan Murdock

Another universe was in his veins.
Flower stem arms of lily white.
A mind of explosives more real than
Half-life conversation made of gold.
Loving eyes full with guns, and he said,
"I was not made for this world."

Jackknife tongue and tenderness.
Shock black hair and micky slips,
The scorch of this age's relentlessness
Dreaming and floating within him.
Another universe was in his veins.
Milk-love hope, bone break games.

Heroin slide and grease dream thought.
Pistol neurons and pollinate hours.
Excavation of mind's spinning top.
A child in innocence crushing power.
Love ripped and fused to the soul, he said,
"I was not made for this world at all."

Pan to the lights blazing above a city.
Pan to the garbage-hoarding gutter crawls.
Pan to the bars with lush word-smithies.
Pan to the human race against time's wall.

Pan to the flesh dancers in red lights.
Pan to desire wearing ripped thread tights.

He had attitude, the breaking of clear glass pain,
Snarl the wind beat of the trees,
Mick Jagger lips and off-cuff name
Slipping from language in the street.
Stagger and haul, pure or perverse:
In his veins another universe.

Lust shaking the crooks out from his eyes.
Villainy and mayhem and chaos tricks.
Lightning when the heroin in him cries
"Another, another jolt me back like this!"
Hope in the after-glaze of pure gold.
"I was not made for this world."

Perfect Entropy

One word can break a person the same way it builds.
So we live the perfect entropy of imperfect language,
As if this mirror was life, or breath castle's stone,
As if we could say love and love be flesh in a word:
Flesh emoting through the page the temperature
Of a sun blazing on the other side of our tyranny.

Poets work in strange ways. Poetic tyranny
Even stranger. To forget the possible—that history has built
Cities of emotions, our belief at temperatures
Vibrating god, our souls emitting living language,
The genome, a map of our flesh made word:
I assure you that a written stone may be real stone.

For who hasn't brought to the page the actual stone?
History's ghosts work around disbelief's tyranny,
Distorts us into pain, fear, hate, and love is broken in a word,
Wars waged, lives made. The sound image slowly builds
And the mirrors shift the power of language.
Taste and wince at the written lemon, 'temperature'

Burn through to the reader's bone, temperature
To brand us deep as conception! Feel here the cold stone,
Fruit that has dropped to a ground of ink, language
That has broken what disbelief was, the tyranny
Made impossible by a child who builds
A castle out of crushed mountains on the beach, word

That exposes the spoken beauty of love 'in-words'.
All the while, theophany raises the vital temperature
Of poetry to heat flickering through time and builds
A literate body as durable as stone
Born by the mouth in love saying, "for we are nothing, tyranny,
If the word love is not living in a living language."

Burn me at the temperature of the stars. Breathe life
Into the word stone. Build a city out of language and then
Let tyranny be the perfection of my madness.

Gambling

For Marc Berger

All the faces are lit with lights
And dreams will gamble with their nights
    When they sleep.
But they won't sleep because endlessness
Has laid its bets and relentlessness
    Has made its leap.

The fingers that hold the chips hold fate
By a tenuous threads while cards are laid
    On the table.
Marry my queen with a king
Give me an ace and I'll sing
    While I'm able.

And around the surround of machines
Coins are popped, faces stream
    With lucky smiles.
Or sweat when you are down a bill,
Or grand sweats when you have nil,
    No plucky wiles.

You want the dealer as much as love
To break every time while above
    The lenses watch.
You want the veins of gambling

To make you, take you rambling
        Tense as knots.

Or unwind and blow your smoke away
Around the heads and lights that sway,
        Like flashy puppets.
Who holds the strings? It is your life,
And pit boss smiles gleam like knives,
        What's in your pockets?

Erase me here. Dive into time.
Hope you get your purse back and dime
        In the end.
Begin again in fear. Dive into lust
For the cards that come up and bust,
        Never lend.

And so many nights, it is no different,
The tables are stables, the cards presents
        That mesmerize.
You sit down and crack your wallet
And then no going back, just pull it,
        The human prize.

So you go to unwind, to play it light,
Games galore that suck the night,
        Vampire-esque.
The thing is, you will lose in the end,
The family, house, love and friend,
        The house's best.

43

Addiction could not be sweeter,
Like a cocktail up or neater
        To quaff down.
Addiction of what you cannot guess,
Not knowing playing you the best,
        Like sloppy clowns.

So hold me and keep the rent my love
For I'll go back and get bent my love
        Into debt.
This is the end. This is confession
And gambling has made its impression,
        I was swept.

The Chain Gang

They broke the rock with more than pick.
Crack! swing low by the blistering sun,
The breaking building them when they hit.

History of hammer. History of pain. Swing low don't quit
My body now! They swung down iron's hardest song,
Breaking the rock with more than pick.

Heavy, each stroke of time, and down they swung it
Though the master said, "you'll never be done,"
The breaking building them when they hit.

Pain, who could carry this load? Swing low don't quit
Me now hand, for death is master holding gun.
They broke the rock with more than pick.

Each breath a rasp from the lung, the chariot
Coming for to carry them home,
The breaking building them when they hit.

Church, God, lift me now to see the spirit!
History struck me with its heavy bone:
They broke the rock with more than pick,
The breaking building them when they hit.

Upon the Tracks

As the train pulls through the city
    After midnight has tucked us in,
Our dreams are almost as pretty
    As the crookedness of sin.

The sin of rivers sweeping
    Towns into the sea,
The sins of little children
    Who were once you and me.

And innocence sits in the corner
    Of all the adult minds,
Because they have witnessed war,
    Fought for ages chains of time.

Because they would crack the spell
    That took away their youth,
Because growing we have our hell
    Of which Heaven is the root.

So a lover steps on the tracks
    As the train moves through the town,
Earthquake heart that cracks
    As he lays his body down.

Because we have turned away

And because we have ignored,
The world cannot say,
   The right words were never scored.

The man lies their feeling nations
   Within the his dusty hands,
Worlds he could have lived in
   Not broken by demands.

And as the light comes closer
   He cannot tell apart
The shaking of the metal
   Or the shaking of his heart.

His eyes are closed and gripping,
   His hands are moon bone white
Under starlight that's tipping
   The universe into night.

And just as the tracks are quaking,
   The train and whistle shrill,
He remembers what he was making
   When a child still.

A boat made out of balsa,
   A sail made out of cloth,
A lake with light and water
   Delicate as a moth.

And he rises like this vision
   As if a man reborn,

And the train and his decision
    Sail past like thunderstorm.

The train pulls through the city
    As he turns and walks for home,
One memory that gave him living,
    Yesterday moving bone.

And all the stars above him
    Quiver constellation light,
As his ideas regarding sin
    Disperse into the night.

For the world is as changing
    As an ocean beach of sand,
Life and death rearranging
    The fates by human hand.

And so sin you may beguile us,
    And hope you may return,
One piece of dust defile us,
    The point is to learn.

New Years Eve, 2001/2

January light knocks at the door,
All the leaves are scattered on the floor
  Like butterflies.
The year has passed almost as surely
As their fall in gravity's purely
  Ancient eyes.

We celebrated, swam in the glass,
Recited poems as if our last
  Hope in the world.
We made resolutions in our hearts,
Gave up our innards to body parts,
  So we were told.

A game of dominoes, a nod and wink,
Hootchi coochie that was the stink,
  Or so they said.
We passed it round saying nice mon
In almost perfect Rastafarian,
  Went to our head.

Now things get hazy, but I remember
That all the speeches became embers
  To light the room.
Rich said Jackson's hair was lightening,
A double entendre surely as exciting

As landing on the moon.

We discussed transplant games, what they were,
And Rich told us: the Olympic other
     For new organs.
I posed a question related,
"Do they play this in such states as
     Oregon."

We chuckled after and took sips
From Guinness bottles at our lips
     And laughter.
Jackson wanted to play with maps
And held them rolled in his hand that
     Swept the rafters.

The Itol was great and went down
As surely as we clowned around
     About ourselves.
We discussed the advent, a new CD
Coming out of the machine perfectly
     As music wells.

But this was it, we had all passed
The millennium that was echoing last
     Year.
And now we wanted something better,
Celebration of our antimatter,
     Free air.

That is, we were looking towards

A time that would carry our words
    To the stars.
Or was it, rather, that we expected
This one to be the best, better erected
    Than our pars?

Anyway, we celebrated
That even though we weren't related
    We could be.
At least we were all human here,
And soul eased in the room as clear
    As we were free.

And at the hour, though in different places,
I imagined one billion crystal glasses
    Clinking.
And the moment after this moment passed
All the merriment of world amassed,
    Drinking.

The Changelings

Somebody has broken a fish in space
And all the scales are scattered stars.
That our atmosphere sees them in butterflies
Is the grip of the rain that broke the skies;
Is the tip of the scales on an angel's face;
Is the vision-broken-window of our stars;
Is the shuddering mystery of this place.

A mobile hangs from this ceiling
And the child that blows it is the wind.
That he was only making love with butterflies
Is the innocence of air that bears the skies;
Is the presence messaging and its singing;
Is the once-worm-laughter of cocoon wind;
Is the rippling pond's breath and edges clinging.

The gravity of the image soaks his heart
And the lion drinks water from the pool.
That space would watch them in butterflies
Is the changeling drama of the skies;
Is the mask that Nature wears to impart;
Is the refracted-game to feed the king's fool;
Is the perfect machine speaking art.

Somebody has invented all of the petals
And just by looking these airports.

That a city of children laugh in butterflies
Is the pretty-tongue-festival of the skies;
Is the brook that looks like flowing metal;
Is the haphazard-sovereignty once had in courts;
Is the tea, the cup, water, flame and kettle.

To rest here, to rest here, to be a tourist
And see for the first time a waking dream.
That hour tells the day we all are butterflies
Is the time we can break open in the skies;
Is the mark on the aether-page that is the surest;
Is the flint-frictioned-spark that meets water, still beams;
Is the hope we could ask for in the purist.

And another has made the ocean a room
And within the silence a place to live.
That the currents would be called butterflies
Is that they are also space, stars, laughter and skies;
Is the utter potential changing all that's spoken;
Is the holism bearing across to give;
Is the magic, the dream, the living, and question.

Deadpan

Nouning Around

It is gone, as usual, the beginning noun
Requisite for making this a good poem.
Something like "Face" or "Sand" or "Clown"

That could have ruled this circus. In
The back room in smoking chairs
The other poets are gurgling, laughter

Barely able to contain itself. I,
Embarrassed, am an earthquake again
Shuddering and infected by such affairs.

It could have been good, something solid,
Like "Table" or "Stone" or even "Bug."
It could have lived in its person and place

And the thing part could have chugged
Down a whole bottle of wine. Now,
However, abstraction works in the sweatshop

Terceted poetic room, disgusted by
Personification, stitches one plug
Into a jacket, one pregnancy into a moon

And throws in the cow.

Eleven Different Ways to Understand Patience

Wait long enough and everything clears
Leaving nobody around save your virtue.

Just another way of saying, "so",
In a conversation that doesn't "go".

Really a pause that has gone awry,
Forgot there is at the end of time "die".

An intersection where everyone
Is doing Tai Chi when green goes on.

One stone. The stone's mother. The stone's great
    grandfather,
The great great grandfather of the stone…earth.

A man on a date with a woman who talks.
The date on the calendar that didn't stop.

Molasses divided the waters and the people
Of the Kingdom passed through.

An elevator in a poem about love.
Then I realized we were going…down.

A pun taking a stroll in the future.
Nobody takes notice, save the thrill.

An aphorism that not even a chisel could bust.
A bust that not even a chisel could aphorism.

Trafficking rush hour until your words slur.
Trying to get back to your story after.

Wasting Time in a Poem

To waste time properly in a poem—
Wait, let me tie my shoe—you must
Have a grasp of—hold on a second,
The light's not right—audience trust,
That straight to the heart sale—pardon,
I am receiving a call—like that beacon
On the shelves in supermarkets where—
There is more room in the back—the sudden
Colors of a package stand out—I am getting
To the point, if you'll be patient—so beautiful
That you must buy it but have to stand—
If you are uncomfortable I'll slow—in line
With the rest of the customers—I mean, really,
If you are getting fidgety I will pause—time
In your mind like sludge taffy turning—signs
Can be confusing, a footnote then, this is about
My dog—your patience into blistering heat—
He was a really nice dog actually, a Terrier—
Your foot tapping, your hands sweating, shout
So loud inside that—do you feel what I am saying?—
You scream until the register breaks—Oh, did
I tell you that one about the kid with the kazoo—
And the rest of the customers look at you,
(Dramatic Pause) and you have to swipe your card
That's over used—I suppose this is not going to be
Published—and your credit is shot and the others—

Please god deliver me from my sins and this reading—
Begin to fidget like popcorn in pans, their oily stares—
Does anybody have a match?—wilt on your body
And you go home to flesh out another reality—
Shall I continue?

Like You Know

California's sorority cheer
Celebrates an evening of underwear.
(We're under wear) just from hearing,
The colloquial gift something searing
As My God! in every sentence—
There is no possible lingual penance.
Like you know.

Lucy squiggles in her low cut pants
Some hybrid sexual thong-tight dance
While applying dark lash seductives,
Mascara stroked, the eruptive
Vermilion lipstick like cherries.
She gazes, blooms and somewhat marries
Herself, like you know.

Suzan within the same glass mirror
Gossips on about how clearer
She sees herself after being fixed,
Tit-pumped silicon to raise the dicks
Out for the hunt, body detection,
My God, like it's like perfection,
Like you know.

And in the same toilet room
Beatrice the cat applies some moon-

Soft powder to her Hellenic face,
Blemish hidden for the 'die herd's' pace
When the surfers come in and say like dude.
Her mini-skirt almost makes her nude
Like you know.

Madonna pumps from the machine
Which they bop to, pretend and dream
That they were she, project Monroe
As they toss their heads to and fro
To perfect the mating dance, the eyes
Glitter-full, the almost trance. My,
Like you know.

A conversation: Lucy says,
"Bobby has been coming," says,
"He's like so hard for me, duh,
Doesn't he like know the treat, ah,
Is like Beatrice. I mean, really,
Boys are just so like silly
My god!"

Beatrice looks up from her powder
And says shuttt uuup almost louder
Than the hairdryer blimping curls.
"Like doesn't he know," she unfurls
Her best affectation of control,
"He's such a doofus and I'm total. . .
Like you know

Totally out for Jim, the hunk,

He's so cute and stupid when drunk."
"Oh that's sick!" the others scream.
(Indeed, the pun was an erected dream).
They giggle, helium-hi for seconds
Until the mirror to them beckons.
Like you know.

Suzan is in sort of a trance
As she puts on her padded pants,
The kind to, like the rap song cries,
"I like big butts and I can't deny."
"Cool!" says Beatrice and then Lucy,
"You're gonna look like so like floozy,
Like you know."

A switch to Vanilla Ice transpires,
"He's so like nice, like so on fire."
"He's a dream, I would love to go down."
"He's mine you bitch!" Lucy frowns,
And the mirror pauses as they move
To dissing each other just to prove
Like you know.

They're jealous cats. "Beatrice,
If you could have any man, that is,
If you could have any man." "You
Already like said that like," says Su.
"Like all right you cunt," replies B,
Her nickname when personally
Like you know

Trounced. But they move to devastation
Of reducing name to their fashion
Of letter likes, a faster way, communication
That now has them S, L and B,
For B stands for Bitch again,
S for Sassy and L for lame,
Like you know.

But it passes and they are now adorned,
Ready to step into the city porn
And walk like the Spice Girls down the street,
Long nails, glitter, hips to the beat
Of their carnal Twenty Something.
They clear their heads so that nothing
Like you know

Can interfere. Then step out the door
And disappear.

Cell Phone

Everywhere cell phones,
The umbilical to elsewhere,
Cell phones hooked up to heads,
Heads hooked up to skeletons,
Skeletons hooked up to genealogy,
Genealogy hooked up geological.

Everywhere like we have missed
Communication for so long a time,
The natter, the chatter, the spew, the talk,
The effluvium of word, the pissed
Discourse, the rant, the sale, the sublime
Love convos and speech with its list
Of needs. Hooked up to the line,
Hooked up in the line, through the line,
Down the line, out of line, what's a line.
Hooked up from finger punch to stitches
In the satellite's circuits, hovering in space,
Hooked up to the company, to the office,
To the government, to their needs, to faces
So far away the sound supplants body.

Hooked up like heroin addicts,
In our cars, in restaurants, in the bathtub,
In the elevator, on the toilet, in street,
In our veins electrically crunching the numbers.

Hooked so we get our everywhere,
Make the sale, connect, network, rub
Shoulders with, do business, make it happen,
Meet up, set the date, set up the date,
Get our now, get our righteous, get there
So we have our here, so we have our everything.

Hooked up like maggots, syllables flying,
Diction bending, fiction rending, pass
The butter, pass the coin, pass me all,
Pass the email, the text message, pass your mama,
Pass the deal, the shake, the twist, the sudden,
The anima, the random, the cussing, the verb.

Wait, I'm loosing you. It must be a tunnel.
Can you hear me? It must be the battery,
The satellite, the office, the center, the government,
The company, the over there, the chimpanzee operator,
The car transmission, the Western Grid, the snowstorm,
The caller minutes, the cell phone ferries, gremlins,
Because I left her, because I forgot, because I sinned,
Because I didn't pay the bill, because I forgot my name,
Because I'm a fucker, a user, a taker, a breaker.
Can you hear me!

A Woman's Room

Rooms in dreams are usually women.
—Interpretation of Dreams, Freud

She had four walls, two windows,
A door to knock up, one knob to turn,
Some furniture to make sin go
Crawl into the cracks, slowly burn
Itself away until her...couch.

She had a carpet that spoke, no joke,
A shag, that she let you walk on,
Perhaps slip in your soles, poke
In her corners if you had your talk on
That would keep her turning...to the couch.

She had this: pillows that mounded
Up like an ice cream, a double trouble
Toil and lick, the way countries are founded,
A nice dream that made you lay down double
Quick and sink in to that...soft couch.

And if you looked out of her windows,
All of that light rubbing up against glass,
You might see her reflection make sin go
Bi-pass your beating heart, passed
Into the comfort of her...couch.

One could live here for life if the quote isn't wrong,
Tap dance on her floor, boogie in her song,
Slip on the carpet until you went swimming
Warm in the room of a woman that's on…her couch,
Now if rooms in dreams are usually women.

Kneading a Loaf of Bread

And a lightly colored loaf of bread stands for physical nudity.
— Interpretation of Dreams, Freud

I was kneading the physical nudity
On the table, the soft loaf, lightly colored,
In my hands, folding it over, stupidly
Thinking that it was a loaf of bread.

Yet on the table the yeast, the flour,
The stuff going on inside like percolating
Life in the hands of a mother, our
Common connection was the thought

That what I was kneading (physical nudity)
Was not a loaf of bread but the fold
In the knead where the need of all bread
Makers becomes physical nudity.

Over and over and over again (somewhat
Like editing a poem!) the physical
Nudity began to take on form, become that
Smooth round body that one could love

If they knew that it was physical nudity
And not a loaf of bread on the table,
That you would eat later on with soup

And a smile, all that nudity like a loaf

Of well kneaded bread. And you say how
In all the world could a baker mistake
The loaf for physical nudity, and I say,
Because he went to a psychotherapist!

Experimental Music

Foreword

The first section of this tryst I was so depressed that I weighed in at 800 pounds of dejection and broke ground with my spirit. Indeed, these poems were written at a gravity that I hope no one else has to experience. Yet it was a gravity that provided a good brush with the worst possible feelings, and, oddly, those were close enough to give body to perception. Since the duress was sublime (painfully sublime) I knocked them out, one by one, and climbed up a ladder of syllables that forgave me every push of the keys. By the last one—I think it was "Lust"—I knew some things. What I knew was that if poetry takes you down, in verse you may rise. The quality of the poems, however relative, worked. The work and working through figured me…out, out of a terrible weight. In short, these notes on emotion were a writing from the lowest possible place I ever want to go, yet, with feeling, resuscitated me back into a lighter relation with myself. If there is anything that the metaphor of a pearl teaches it is that she is part of the guts of the sea.

Somewhere between knowing this and life there is a lot of experimental music. Miles Davis, probably with sardonic humor, noted, "If you don't know what it is it's jazz", a definition that helps fill up loss with a body of music that is always shifting. Yet 'Experimental Music' is not jazz, however much it shifts, but rather a concoction of 'disarray', pulp diction, dyslexia, 'infusion music', bar blips, lifelines, and 'semantic soda' verbiage that I wanted to shake up. Contrary to 'On Emotions', the poetry came naturally, like children with ice cream, the lick of each piece a focus of attention, spill, and rearrangement until finished. Empirically they struck me as ways in which I might satisfy my desire to be a criminal, the visceral and inspiring American pulp, "I am gonna take your motherfucking money!", somehow so modern. However, contrary to my fascination, I got robbed instead, each poem holding me up, pretty much everyday, until they got what they wanted. Although they stole most of my time, my soul is entirely enthusiastic about the take of such poetic effort. As they got away with the goods I offered them tips—which they also stole—until the poem was satisfied. No time in my life have I been more caring! No time in my experience have I been more creative! The manifestation and coalesce of "good" and "bad" ripped off my belief that good and bad even exist, each poem a lesson in unworldly virtue. Then, in the proverbial words of most writers, I forgave them their singing, kicked them out of the church, and blessed their fiery souls.

Both these renderings are dear to me. I subjected each to the tests of time, critical reading, and association until they could get away safely. Since I am still alive and they have helped, I now want to give them to you to, "make them responsible", a process of reading. And, knowing that nothing is ever finished, I trust you will, with careful reading, hear their echoes. Indeed, if they return—even if they do hold you up—you should get a fair shake. Just give them all your attention/money and love.

Patrick Denton Mackay
October 1, 2008

Anger

She prefers a certain music
With noise tucked deep within

And will slowly make you sick,
Put rage under your skin.

Put words into your mouth
That are hardly ever heard,

Clock you in the jaw so south
You spin back to the word.

And you'll use her to make shadows
Upon all your pretty things,

You'll choose her in the meadows
Where from your love has springs.

And hate yourself a thousand times
For the spit of venom of

The very thing that keeps the times:
This centerpiece of love.

And quietly the simmer cool,
The thrash gone with its spike,

Deep inside you will rule
Yourself with temper's knife.

Baby, it's not laughable
To mend a heart gone mad,

But it's harder to be affable
Than to watch her wilt to sad.

And sadder to be madder
Than a bull with all that red,

You'll get the point and be gladder
Than everything you have said.

Fear

It begins in throat and then ices
The chest on down to gut,

Cracks its whip, but never suffices
To crack its whip enough.

A blanket of unspeakable sickness,
Its vocabulary is large,

Lives in language until witness
Sees the words that it rips apart.

Rips them without any pity
As they tear and tangle one's speech,

Rips like the lights of a city
That can't stop the blaze of its reach.

Yet nothing is there to fight with
And nothing is there save you

And the wicked thing is that like it
Your fight adds fearing to you.

Viscera of unspeakable music,
An opera awkward in heart

And suddenly it is confused with
Beauty and her beauty mark.

It seeps slowly into these eyes,
Puts a pendulum in the stare,

Swings seeing to blindness and tries
To have you love from there.

But come up close and behold it,
Look dead on into its soul

And you see how nothing holds it,
The denial is terrible.

Desire

She is not exactly a snowfall of want
Or a blizzard of must, a hail of need,

But a slink of the think that creeps up front
To your eyes fixated upon her seed.

So your gaze feels and ears go kinetic
And your taste buds perform coup de mouth,

While the nose inhales the scent of her atom,
Hearts beating birds in hot amounts.

Displaces your madness and inserts a tick
That clicks you into her gravity trick.

Spins your clock to a hot midnight,
Long hand on the flesh exact

As the hanging midair swing and flight
Of your hormonal acrobat.

Music like syrup from maple purer
Than the first DNA from your family line.

A melt. A blaze. A beat. A surer
Heart hunting the first tick of time.

Entire countries fall into this creature whose nest
Is the temperature of stars, and oh baby burns!

Entire planets gorging everything lest
Their moon's mythos forget a celestial turn.

Panic

They say there is a button for this agitated beast,
And on Monday—not your funday—it comes screwing up its nose,

Pulls a no key where there should have been a key to say the least
And your mouth begins to mutter crap that no one really knows.

They say there is a panic for every kind of people,
Like an addict with specific type of oil or drink or drug,

A panic for all worshippers now passed and up the steeple
As they climb to God like angels on the glory of their good.

And they say when shit is hitting fans all across the nation
Don't be a fan 'cause then you'll get smeared like puny flies

Who, without a blink do not think and hit windshields a-blazing
One hundred miles an hour without least suicidal try.

Aye panic aint for pussies, nor for wimps or chumps or quacks,
Panic only is for those who know how to fall apart,

Like professional disasters, holes, or large Grand Canyon cracks,
So the depth of panic goes with the scenario like art.

The braker on the freeway, the fantastic fop with words,
The baby on the stairs, the wedding's vocal chords,

The earthquake of all lovers who didn't quite match up,
The post coital mistake of not knowing who is what,

The creep of all governments into one's hearth and home,
The throw up that won't go up, the ache in youthful bones.

But put your panic in the bank and wait just about a year,
Check the balance afterward and you will be surprised

That your panic has gone up, worth more than a queen's tear,
And you tremble in all your love for neurosis, panics' bride.

Greed

How minute greed; how much it takes;
Want too damp a word to be its bride;

For it would take her too and slowly rake
Out everything she had stored up inside.

But not having enough, not possessing all,
Not being satisfied, never getting what

Nobody else has—what bitter fall!
What full stomach would want more gut?

What head with brain need more brain?
What title more title when it has its name?

It steals most from the one who's swinish,
Eats them after the loot is had,

Devours like a gormandizing finish
To a meal where none greedy are too glad

But the greed itself that lives in skull.
And its mirth is jealousy; its love false;

Its joy empty, the decay's slow pull
Of a take replenishing its fake heart.

Were you ever anything sympathetic
Before your vacuum began to suck?

You come now covered with the pathetic
Welcoming word façade. Dumbstruck

The amusement park goers filter in,
Climb onto the turn of time,

Sucking all of happiness in when
Life tells them a moment's left.

Depression

Gut, pure gut, and then heart
Begins to clutch, gripping paper,

The tremor to make you start,
Make you feel your cold maker.

Floats your gag in the harbor of soul,
Puts a stone in mouth to ache it,

Shoves you into your fire like coal,
Burns you cheap until you can't take it.

Smothers in the druthers that you would not
Sway in your ways until freed,

Loves you as much as house rot,
Kicks you out with your own moxie.

And oh her name like bad tonic!
Sweeps you into doing what you can't,

Chucks it all in to the moronic,
No music to make the place dance.

And what a silly thing to take her
Out into the street where your friends

Are happy 'cause they will relate 'er
To the feeling that gives you the bends.

But step up like a poet and kiss her,
Put the word love in her mouth,

Pull her deep into gut and whisper,
You're a bitch but you can live in my house.

'Cause if not depression she will be,
Something with the make of a guess...

Emote, man, all, you're free,
Clog it and they are stopped at the press.

Anxiety

There is a ghost in the girlfriend with whom you sleep,
His lips taste like a blowup doll,

There's a law that you cannot help but cheat:
What she is is what you are.

Relations gone bonkers and busted,
A plant is a plant is a "plant",

Your speech has suddenly rusted
So a will won't and can can't.

You try to rhyme anxiety with piety
And get caught by the Lord of the song

Who tells you what must be sobriety
Otherwise you are doing wrong.

And soon you get stuck in a lift
With an old lady who you must save first,

Her eyes grab you like a gift,
As you grab her thinking the worst.

And in street you pass everybody
Who think you to be a rock star,

You believe their stupidity like shoddy
Things that are left in a bar.

But what gets you anxious the wrong way
Is when you look in the mirror

And see something close to a long way
Away in your eyes that were once clearer.

Baby, she's a matter of life,
Kick back and enjoy the twist,

Everybody's got her like a wife
Married to the love of the gist.

The Vocabulary of Dopamine

For Rich

The drugs speak a different language,
Their time-zone shifty as a fly
Having a smashing time at life's window,
Dopamine vocabulary parachute high,
The float down syllables ticking slur.

Whitewashed, yesterday is a canvas
Ready for its make-up brush.
Did you see it? Did you plan this?
Somewhere neural-time says don't rush;
The world is a flip flop game of blur.

Condensed, the minutes one can almost touch
Play hopscotch until they explode.
You thought you had a key to your pain
But are locked out, feel, don't know,
Know too much, know it all, plummet now,

An unchained sun into ocean.
Was it that you broke when the world showed you
The refined meaninglessness of all jobs?
Was it that disbelief became so true
That you fell into the city's gears?

It was challenging to live in three thoughts at once.

A moment cracked and gravity hit
The tongue that tried to hold love.
A snow fell in your heart until it
Made white your words, their cold proof

Full of multiple meanings, like crystals
Are all a unique shape: "real acts,"
"Real ax," "relax." The echoes distill
Themselves, thank goodness hell's on holiday,
Beats like a dream upon realities door.

1

Empty, the most important word,
Goes unnoticed by the throng.

She fills the cracks in city walls
And makes her body out of wind,

Collects the breath of ending life
From so many mouths that have spoken.

And, toying with the air like a god,
She throws her body upon lonely men;

Shivers out each staple of loss
And succumbs repeatedly to nothing.

What strength in her absent limbs;
What soul in her displaced time.

Somewhere she grasps her maker's pen,
Writes how the world is a broken fable…

Suddenly she loses her body
And a baby sees her in her mother's eyes,

The churches, married to god, feel
The millions of moments where she ached.

How may I end this poem
I ask before I, too, marry her?

"You must realize that I am in your love."

A Minute of Your Time

Time eats until it is empty,
A diminishment of the things around it;
Like decay it is a selfish kiss.

But you can feel it in your bones,
Its brittle vocabulary, a lightness,
The first betrayal for your life.

The quality of knowing wisdom must bear what
Lesson your aging teaches. Slow,
The hours go by, groping, starving

For what innocence time may clutch.
Who do we dance with? What may we know?
She pulls us closer and closer to truth.

She waltzes us closer to accepting
That the next day is a cliff,
That our footsteps, ephemeral as breath,

Will eventually become the air.

5:23 p.m.

In the center of the aloe
The late afternoon sun
Is turning the rain
Into a chalice of sparks.

Occasionally one of the sparks
Falls from the chalice of the aloe
As if on fire a drop of rain
Or a syllable chip of the sun.

The spider webs around in the sun
Quiver with intensity, sparks
Sliding down their thread, rain
On the line feeding the aloe

Light, if light may be eaten. The aloe,
Scintillated, pregnant, bulging with sun
Brilliant as the mere feel of rain
Quivers in the light and eases sparks

Like sun if she could rain and the aloe
If it were a chalice to drink from,
The flicker of a believable Universe.

The No Theater

Leftovers

Nothing is mundane. The feet-pounded dust holds
    bodies,
Bodies that once laughed, intricate, refined bones
That make the roses bloom. I can't.

Say the right words about them, enough about them.
A junkyard with so many tangled wires
Is almost better than language's tangled wires.

This has come from minds and after hands
And after sales and after homes and after gone.
A soul in the bleeding rust, like words. I can't.

Say enough about them. Nothing is mundane.
Down
To earth we have our pain.
Down
To pain we have our lives.
Down
To lives
We have our astonishing upcomings and death.
Down
To death we have anything. I can't.
Say enough about what down to earth means.

Nothing is mundane. The passed over dew,

The crushed grass, the cracked shells on
All the shorelines, the gutter filled with glorious

Trash, trash filled with glorious action. Action
Filled with astonishing discards. Nothing is
Mundane. I can't say enough about this. I can't.

Lake Missing

It is the lake that is not there again,
Not evaporated, but gone, not missed,
But misplaced, not left out, but left

In somewhere that has never been.
Not on a map that's super specific,
Not on tongue told where it had wet

The floor of a valley with reed grass and ducks.
Not in a story with sky glint and shimmer.
Not, you will notice, anywhere in here.

You missed it at the last turn in the diction
On a highway that wasn't anywhere close,
In a state that had been rubbed out by what

It didn't do for itself. You are still looking?
The dusk is heavy with anticipation. Those
Moments of looking remind of other moments.

You cannot take it anymore. You pull over
And break down. Break down? Yes. Lover
Of the lost will not your tears tell you?

Things swim in your eyes!

Deep

I have always been unsure of my love
Whose off-balance words push me over
Like a bully who wants me to know
That when I fall she'll be there.

Since I cannot love the fall
I love the thunder

Of my doubt that there will be ground
To break open the very core of meaning.

I mean meaning when I rest in her eyes
And she tells me it was only a whisper
That lay me flat into her love,
Only a whisper so particular and sacred

That our time
                        Splattered all
Over
          The streets

In a foreign language.

So without malice or guilt

Like a child sent into life's words.

A word in the mouth of love to be,
Just about to say, to be stable, to be
Unstable and say the word able as love to be
On the lips as suddenly as air to be
Unstable and suddenly as a scream, to be
A word in the mouth unstable and necessary
As love to be…

Awakened in her meaning
No matter the thunder; for my life,
Even only a whisper, or even only her words,
Is absolute as a storm.

When Nothing's There

There is nothing outside this window
That could turn a phrase,
As if January's present was the empty
View that one could gaze forever into.

Nothing in the dull green leaves,
The light on them, its infinities,
The slight air breathless as age.
Yet, on the glass itself, there is

One handprint reaching for
Something out there one can't ignore.
The strangeness in it makes it live,
Each thin line catching light,

Or up as if to say stop and hold!
And then nothing has importance too.
Who knows when or how old
It is, the mark of some workman who

Wanted to spackle the surrounding frame.
It remains there curious as a name
One used to know but lost.
How long has it held the oak,

Or the glass where it is pressed?

How long can it save the light
That strikes it, no, lights it like
Skin slick after a bath? And who

Will soak themselves longest, question,
Get lost and then found when they ask?
It is dead still. It is what is left. It is when
We forget to see the detail that being

Loses the grasp on itself, the holding
That, like trust, holds one on.
The print exhibits where something's from,
The leaves appear around the molding.

www.ingramcontent.com/pod-product-compliance
Lightning Source LLC
Chambersburg PA
CBHW051843040426
42447CB00006B/665